Kings & Priests

by

David R. High

Books for Children of the World

6701 N. Bryant,

Oklahoma City, OK 73121

Kings & Priests

by

David R. High

Books for Children of the World

6701 N. Bryant,

Oklahoma City, OK 73121

Distributed by:
Books for Children of the World
6701 N. Bryant
Oklahoma City, OK 73121
voice - 405/721-7417
fax - 405/478-4352

Printed in the United States of America

Table of Contents

INTRODUCTION

When I was a boy of five, God would talk with me regularly on the phone at night in my dreams. As I lay sleeping, the phone would ring and when I would answer, it would be God. During one of our conversations, God called me into His ministry in a very personal and dramatic way. His words have stayed with me for the last 42 years. His words were that my service to Him would be different than anything I could perceive the ministry to be. You may think that at five my idea of ministry would be fairly limited, and it wouldn't take much to have God's words fulfilled. At that time, I had been in church every Sunday since I was two weeks old. It was a small but active church. Even at such an early age, I sang specials, took up the offering, and attended revivals with my mother, who played the organ. Church was the center of our lives.

For years after my childhood message, it remained a puzzle as to how my service to God could be significantly different than what I continued to experience week after week. The pastor preached, the choir sang, the offering was taken, revivals came and went. At 19, God reaffirmed my ministerial call. At 21, I attended Bible college and after graduation was invited to join the staff of a large church. By age 25, I had traveled abroad in mission work, taught several years in a Bible school, helped start and administrate a Christian day school, conducted home Bible studies, and had started a new church. While all of this was quite exciting, I could not say that any of those things met the criteria of being significantly different than I thought the ministry would be.

I pastored my own church until I was 39. Now at 47, my experiences with successes and failures have been a glorious journey that has finally led me to the fulfillment of God's challenging promise to a young boy 42 years ago. This small book is my attempt to shine the light of God's understanding on a different way of living. These words are written with the prayer for you to find challenges that will change your life.

A Disservice to the Men of God

A friend of mine once said, "You can't take people somewhere you have never been." The older I get, the more I appreciate the profoundness of that statement. Having pastored for over 20 years, I found that when my turn came to give direction to a body of believers, I simply reproduced what I had seen for years as my example from my pastors. I planned programs at the church as if no one had anything else to do but support what I dreamed up. Once, after reading a book on evangelism, I created evangelistic outreaches for our church. When the whole church didn't rally to support my latest bright idea, I found myself being critical and, in my mind, accusing the members of apathy.

Periodically, I would re-teach messages of great teachers on finances. After brief financial responses from the congregation, the giving would settle back to previous levels. Once again, I viewed this as apathy. I tried every trick I knew to inspire, motivate, even manipulate the saints into action. One thing that never occurred to me, however, was that my congregation simply didn't have a clear understanding of the big picture - the vision God was giving to me. Rather, I preached inspiring and anointed messages. These were disjointed, unrelated, stand-alone masterpieces that were jerking the people in this direction and that. There were no clearly defined, biblically based goals to be the signposts or to give direction and coordination to my anointed ramblings on subject after subject.

I would read the Bible to get a message _for_ Sunday rather than to get a message _from_ God. Oh, I convinced myself that God was speaking through me, but I lacked clear direction that gave me confidence that I was taking the congregation someplace that was pleasing to God. I lived with the continual frustration that the people weren't committed. Even though I myself couldn't answer the question, "Committed to what?" It was that elusive "what?" that drove me to program after program, as I tried to find the magical equation to build a dynamic, explosive, successful and happy group of believers.

Several years ago my life took on a dramatic change. God moved me from the pulpit to the marketplace. Talk about culture shock. Suddenly, all the clichés and statements of faith I had laid on the men of my church were tested in my arena of reality. I found that the

4

business world was not as black and white as it had seemed from behind the pulpit. I found the opposition to my success to be far more vicious than anything I had encountered in the ministry. My creativity was challenged to its limits. It was as if hell was more threatened by my financial success than it was by my spiritual success. For several years, I searched the Word and questioned the Lord in every way I could to find the answers to my destiny.

Now that I was in the pew and not in the pulpit, one of the first things that was made real to me was how extremely difficult it was for me to live up to the same expectations I had tried to put on the men of my congregation. While a pastor, I had little appreciation for the difficulties men had in running businesses, leading their families, while at the same time, trying to support all the ministries and programs of the church. When I pastored, I wondered why men didn't come on Tuesday nights for choir practice, Wednesday nights for Bible study, Thursday nights for evangelism, and Saturday mornings for prayer. Now that I was one of those businessmen, I never seemed to be able to work it all into my schedule either. I began to have deep feelings of inadequacy and guilt, just as I am sure the men of my congregation must have felt. As a pastor, I continually looked for reassurance that I was doing a good job by the level of commitment I could coerce out of the men. All the while, the men must have felt as I now did. They could never quite live up to the expectations.

If one of the men ever did have a burst of exceptional service, the standard practice was to encourage him to go to Bible school and become a youth director. Now it began to dawn on me that the expectation of the Church in many cases was misplaced and unfair. We always needed more money for our expanding--often disjointed--ministries of the Church. All the while, we were heaping guilt on the men who could be supplying the resources by insisting, if they weren't at every church function, they were apathetic to the things of God. If someone seemed exceptionally successful financially, we stripped him of his success and sent him off to minister, thus negating His pure gift from God. What a crazy system. Guilty, frustrated men were trying their best to keep up with unrealistic expectations to please guilty pastors who created more and more programs to please God. There had to be a better way.

How Did Israel Function?

I believe God's wisdom in the structure of Israel is something that can help us in the New Testament Church. Revelation 1:6 says that we will be kings and priests unto our God. In Israel, kings and priests were two distinct and different offices.

Let's look at the roles of priests and kings.

Priests:

1. Carried the responsibility of hearing from God.

2. Offered sacrifices for the people.

3. Received tithes and offerings from the people.

4. Cared for the house of God.

5. Cared for the widows and orphans.

6. Cared for the stranger at the gate.

7. Spoke encouragement to the people before battle.

Kings:

1. Destroyed the enemies of God.

2. Took the spoils of war.

3. Paid tithes and offerings to the priests.

4. Governed the physical affairs of the nation.

Even though priests were from time to time involved in government as advisors, they didn't stir the people to overthrow bad kings. Rather, they spoke the word of the Lord over the situation and eventually judgment came. While kings at times gave directly to the needs of people, they were not permitted to interfere with the priest's office. In fact, if a king tried to do a priest's job, he suffered judgment from the Lord.

Once when Saul was impatient to go into battle, he stepped over the line when Samuel was delayed. The priest was to offer sacrifice and pronounce blessing over the people before battle (Deut. 20:1-4). When Samuel was late, Saul made the sacrifice himself and invalidated his office of king. Samuel said to Saul, *What have you done?* (I Samuel 13:11). The event was so out of place for a king that Samuel pronounced this word of judgment against Saul: *But now your kingdom shall not continue* (I Samuel 11:14).

While some minor common ground was permitted, the lines of separation were pretty firm. Some things were simply not permitted. This separation brought great respect for both offices. The king wouldn't go to war without the priest's blessing. The priest wouldn't have anything to distribute to bless the nation without the king's success in battle.

Priests Provided Vision;
Kings Provided Provision

A divine teamwork coexisted for centuries in Israel. Mutual respect born out of mutual need. The priests spoke blessing or judgment to the kings, and the kings dared not harm the priests. When King David sinned with Bathsheba, and Nathan, the prophet, came to him with a word of judgment, David accepted the word and gave no harm to the priest. You can read this account in II Samuel 12: 1-15. In fact, when Solomon was later born, it was this same prophet Nathan who was called by David to bless his new son (II Samuel 12:25). For either to take it upon himself to physically remove the other from office would bring the wrath of heaven. They respected the anointing and calling of God on the office, even when the man failed his office. If God selected, then only God must reject and remove.

Another interesting point is that when God chose the tribe of Levi to be His priests, He split the tribe of Joseph into two tribes--Ephraim and Menassah--which still left twelve other trib.s besides the priests (Numbers 1). Also, Levi was smaller than the other tribes, which meant in the giving of tithes and offerings, there were approximately 27 men tithing for every priest. This structure provided ample supply for the priests to care for their responsibilities listed earlier.

It has always taken financial resource to run the Kingdom and it always will. If the Levites had tried to take all the truly committed men of Israel and make priests out of them, they would have severely upset the balance between vision and provision. It would have been silly for the tribe of Levi to try to make the other 12 tribes feel guilty because they weren't priests. The priesthood wasn't God's destiny for the other tribes. They were the warriors, the providers, the protectors of the nation.

New Testament Application

Please hear me out on this point. I know that we are a royal priesthood and that we shall rule and reign. We are all to some degree both kings and priests. But could it be that as a matter of call or emphasis that we may lean or be bent more to one side than the other? Could it be that the call to provision could be just as important and equally viewed by God as the call to receive the vision? Can we all have a pulpit ministry? If we did, who would the pay the bills?

By living in different seasons of my life on both sides of this fence, I have found there are indeed two separate anointings, one for kings and another for priests. Preparing to conduct a healing crusade and preparing a business presentation require you to draw strength from God differently. In the same way that warriors and priests required different strengths and talents, I believe that the Church today needs to develop all its muscles.

I believe that the modern church has, through ignorance of other options, created subtle pressure to make priests out of every member. Consequently, we have become a kingdom of priests, not kings and priests.

The Church suffers today for lack of long-range planning and provision because the king's side of the Kingdom is severely underdeveloped. Kings are made to feel as second class citizens because they haven't surrendered all and moved to some remote jungle to preach. This lack of honor and recognition has left the 27 providers feeling as if they are failures spiritually and thereby don't see themselves as needed, valuable, and necessary to the fulfillment of God's plan on earth. Unfulfilled kings become spectators and eventually drop outs because they can't find their place.

I believe that the call of God to the king's side of the Kingdom is just as real and necessary as the call to the priest's side. If pastors today understood this simple concept and ministered encouragement to their kings, they would not lose the respect of the people. Rather than lose respect, I believe that divine teamwork would create more powerful, more effective churches that could minister in a more relevant way to their communities and eventually to the world. Kings would have more respect for their priests because they would be free, blessed, and sent to war for the Kingdom.

Fulfilled Kings

God made men to thrive on conquest. When men see their daily lives as being vitally important to the Kingdom's success on planet Earth, something changes inside them. When Monday through Friday is as big a spiritual experience as Sunday, then we are making progress. For the kings of the Kingdom of God, today's battlefield is the marketplace. When men catch the vision that they are going to war to do exploits for God as providers of the Kingdom, real life focus occurs. However, when men see the Kingdom as a weekend thing that doesn't relate to their work, their need for conquest gets misplaced. When kings are not given proper vision to battle as providers, their need for conquest will spin off to other things. You may recall an example of this misplaced conquest from the Bible. When King David should have been in battle with his men, he was at home with time on his hands. Had he been planning his battles rather than planning his pleasures, the incident with Bathsheba may have never happened. You can read the account in I Samuel 11:1-4.

Kings of today with misplaced conquest may take up hang gliding, hunting, alcohol, sexual improprieties, etc., that could eventually lead them out of the Kingdom.

The pastor asks, "Where is George?"

A possible response, "Oh, he is on a hunting trip."

If priests could more effectively show their congregations how to tie their dreams and talents together with Kingdom vision, the people would never live a dull life. The reason George is hunting and not worshiping with the saints is because he is searching for a way to fulfill his need for excitement and conquest. Believe me, there is nothing more exciting or rewarding than tying into a vision from God and seeing it move forward. Believers, not only will your life be filled with God's challenges, but you will find you have less and less time for self-pity, self-indulgence, or other sins.

Sin usually requires a lot of planning, time, thought, and money. When your life is harnessed for the Kingdom, you need not look elsewhere to find fulfillment. *Take My yoke upon you and learn of Me...for My yoke is easy, and My burden is light* (Matt. 11:29-30). To be faithful and responsible, I simply don't have the time or desire to run off and pick up a lot of new, expensive habits.

Could you imagine Moses saying, "Oh, this job is okay I guess, but I think I would have been happier if God had given me Aaron's job."? Moses was on the king's side and Aaron on the priest's. What we often fail to understand is that both were spiritual men who were equally anointed to do their jobs. Could you imagine God calling a man to do a job for the Kingdom and not anointing him to do that job? If you want to be anointed, simply submit to the call of God on your life.

Stay in Your Calling

If I can be permitted to oversimplify for emphasis, priests tend to generate vision faster than they generate provision. Since priests are the ears and heart of God to the people, they generally hear the directions and timings of God before others do. This gifting puts them out in front in leadership where vision is concerned. But as we all know, vision almost always requires money to make the vision happen. The priests see that a harvest of souls is coming and they want to build buildings, hire staff, print training materials, etc. Because the king's side of the Kingdom is underdeveloped, the priests start talking more about what is missing (the provision) than they do about the vision. The kings who have been made to feel alienated, unneeded, and guilty that they are not more committed, have withdrawn their heart and see what is going on as the **pastor's** vision. In Israel where the divine team of kings and priests cooperated together, the king heard the word of the Lord through the priest as **God's** vision.

Today we have churches full of frustrated kings, sitting in pews with their arms folded, listening to frustrated priests who have heard from God but don't have the money to make it happen. This creates all kinds of problems. Priests wrongly conclude that the people don't care. They have a mandate from heaven to fulfill what they have heard. What are they going to do?

Priests in this position tend to press the people for more and more money. Because this is not the order or way God has set up His kingdom to work, many priests get out of their calling, become overly money conscious, get in the flesh, and try to become the provisionary themselves. Surely, I don't have to remind you about the many examples from today's church concerning the abuses of money.

Many good, godly men have destroyed themselves and their ministries when they felt they had to become fund raisers. Once they start chasing money, something twists inside and their message and ministry begin to ring hollow. Having crossed the line, they open the door to other abuses and sins. The people say, "All he ever talks about is money." With confidence lost, the spiral of separation between pastors and congregations begins. The pastors and teachers of our day need to see another possible answer to the question, "Why isn't this working?" After all, they have heard a word from God. Where is the provision?

Develop Your Kings

If we could go to Deut. 17:14-20, we find there some clear direction in choosing kings.

When you are come unto the land which the Lord your God gives you and shall possess it and shall dwell therein, and shall say, I will set a king over me, like as all the nations that are about me; You shall in any wise set him king over you, whom the Lord your God shall choose: one from among your brothers shall you set king over you: you may not set a stranger over you, who is not your brother.   But he shall not multiply horses to himself, nor cause the people to return to Egypt, to the end that he should multiply horses: forasmuch as the Lord has said unto you that you shall henceforth return no more that way.   Neither shall he multiply wives to himself, that his heart turn not away: neither shall he greatly multiply to himself silver and gold. And it shall be, when he sits upon the throne of his kingdom, that he shall write him a copy of this law in a book out of that which is before the priests the Levites: And it shall be with him, and he shall read therein all the days of his life: that he may learn to fear the Lord his God, to keep all the words of this law and these statutes, to do them: That his heart be not lifted up above his brothers, and that he turn not aside from the commandment, to the right hand, or to the left: to the end that he may prolong his days in his kingdom, he, and his children, in the midst of Israel.

When priests in their instruction to the Church include the king's office as an option of legitimate God consecrated service, and men see that office clearly; the Kingdom of God on earth will go through a radical transformation. When the honor and respect is offered to the king's side that the priests expect on their side, teamwork of heavenly appointment will emerge. King David never once complained that he had to go beat up the enemies of God and bring back provision for Israel. The priests honored his office and cooperated with him for Israel's success.

What Happens to Kings Who Do Not Have a Proper Relationship with Priests?

Kings who do not have a proper relationship with priests become a law unto themselves, not submitting to the vision of God. How does this happen? Because kings generate provision faster than they generate vision, they are to be the natural leaders in that arena. How many millions of dollars in provision have been wasted because priests and kings don't have proper relationships? Priests simply don't carry the same anointing in finances as kings do. It just isn't their job. They make foolish decisions in finances with the kings watching. Many Christian businessmen have watched the fiscal irresponsibility of the Church and wrongly concluded that these men couldn't possibly be hearing from God. They think, "How could I follow a pastor who says he hears from God and yet makes so many stupid decisions with God's money?" The kings stop giving. They withdraw their hearts. *For where your treasure is, there will your heart be also* (Matt. 6:21). I have found that where your treasure isn't, there your heart isn't either.

When I pastored, I could always tell months before a family left that they were on their way out because their giving fell off and then quit completely. Their heart began to be drawn other places because of the process described above. If you don't feel a part of something, you can't keep giving forever. Eventually, the awkwardness and separation will cause a change.

Another sad consequence of poor king-priest relationships is that kings will reject the priest's vision. If they are generating provision without proper vision, then the wealth is wasted by men born for conquest with no war to fight. *Where there is no vision, the people perish...* (Prov. 29:18a). We have all seen men who make large sums of money and who could make a difference in the progress of the Kingdom, but choose not to. They haven't yet learned the difference between stewardship and ownership. We will discuss that fuller later on. When that happens, this inborn desire for conquest will drive men instead to become workaholics, alcoholics, sportsaholics, sexaholics, etc. The world calls this a mid-life crisis. I can tell you without any doubt, however, this is not a mid-life crisis, but rather a lack-of-vision crisis.

If a man has found his place as a king and has right relationships with priests, it will be all he can do to keep up with his God given wars to fight to bring provision to the Kingdom. There is no time to sit down at 40 and whine about lost youth. I can't remember once in the last 25 years getting up one single morning and wondering, "What will I do today?". The Kingdom challenges me every day to my limits as a steward to be all I can be.

Rejected Kings

What happens when a king loves God yet has been rejected by priests or has come to the wrong conclusion that the priests couldn't possibly be hearing from God? In the same way that priests, who don't enjoy the provision of kings, can pervert their ministry and get them chasing money; kings, who have all this love for God and drive to produce wealth yet have no heaven authorized vision, will sometimes create a vision of their own and hope that they can somehow get God to bless it. Christian businessmen should be careful that their zeal doesn't begin to fight an undeclared war or try to produce an organization born out of a good idea.

Remember, kings trying to be priests may get themselves into trouble. In many cases, the Saturday night Christian businessmen's dinner is nothing more than a church service at a restaurant run by a bunch of unappreciated, frustrated, misplaced kings. Sometimes these meetings become more important for these me than fellowship with the local church and support of a heaven-born vision. The rejection by the Church of the valid ministry of kings within the church structure has forced kings outside and left the Kingdom incomplete and divided.

Priests without kings chase provision to their own hurt. Kings without priests try to generate vision many times to their own hurt. Without money, priests can't fulfill their God-given heart's desire. Without proper direction, kings sacrifice themselves on the altar of their own lusts. What irony and relief. God doesn't want any big shots or lords over each other in His kingdom. *For, brothers, you have been called unto liberty; only use not liberty for an occasion to the flesh, but by love serve one another* (Galatians 5:13). When kings and priests are joined properly, the result is divine teamwork that can only find fulfillment through respect and cooperation.

Stewardship Not Ownership

Deut. 8:18 says that it is the Lord your God who gives you power to get wealth, that He might establish His covenant.

When God allowed Jesus to die for us, there were multiple provisions established for those who believe in Christ 's substitute death for our sins. Forgiveness of sins, healing, health, emotional well being are all promised to those who believe. Many believers are so convinced of these promises that they will storm hell's gates to claim their rightful inheritance. Nothing will deter them in their quest for covenant living. But somehow, when it comes to money, the message and motive seem to get blurred. What is the proper response? Should we stand as firmly, fighting by faith to acquire money as we do to acquire healing or to appropriate forgiveness? After all, God's word says in I Tim. 6:10a, "For the love of money is the root of all evil..." and in Mark 10:25, "It is easier for a camel to go through the eye of a needle, than for a rich man to enter into the kingdom of God." But let's delve a little further.

In Matt. 25:14-30, Jesus taught a parable of the three stewards. To refresh your memory, one was given five talents, one was given two talents, and the last one was given one talent. If God is no respecter of persons, why didn't the master give each steward 3 1/2 talents? It states that He gave to each one severally according to his ability. Now if we convert a talent into today's money, it would be approximately $2,000,000.00. The master must have had great confidence in those three men to entrust them with such wealth. However, he obviously trusted some more than others. The only conclusion that we can come to is that some had more experience, a better track record, something that set them apart.

Stewardship means that you are taking care of somebody else's assets as if they were your own. You don't own the wealth, but you are to care for it as if it were yours. How this concept is like our lives. All that we have is on loan from God. How can we boast in anything we accomplish? Even the reasoning ability we have to make wise decisions comes from God. So as stewards, how are we to handle the Master's investment in us? In Matt. 25:19, the stewards after a period of time, were called to give an account of their stewardship. The first steward, who obviously had the confidence of his master, appeared with 10 talents ($20,000,000). That's a 100% return on the master's investment. If we told most Christians that we had made an investment and doubled our money, they would think we were dealing drugs or involved in some other illegal activity. What was the master's response? Paraphrased, he said, "Good job, you faithful servant; let me reward you." The master was pleased with the return. I would be too with a $10,000,000 profit.

How did the steward make that kind of money? The Word says he took the master's money and put it at risk. *Then he who had received the five talents went and traded with the same, and made them other five talents* (Matt 25:16). He invested it. He took a chance that he might lose it in order to multiply it. Many of us take what we consider to be **our own money** and put it into investments. We then worry and pray over it that God will bless it so we can prosper. When prosperity comes, we thank God that we have been smart and made ourselves some more money. It wasn't ours to start with. It isn't ours now. And we certainly aren't taking any of it with us when we leave here. The only thing that makes sense is to learn the covenant of stewardship so that when we leave here to give an account, we may gain our Master's approval. *His lord said unto him, Well done, you good and faithful servant; you have been faithful over a few things, I will make you ruler over many nations; enter you into the joy of your lord* (Matt. 25:21).

The second steward did the same. He invested two talents and made two more talents. When he appeared before his master, he presented the four talents. Likewise, the master was pleased. Now answer me truthfully. If you were the master, what would you do with your money? Obviously, you would leave it in the capable hands of your trusted servants so that they could continue to multiply your investment. If I told you I had a stock broker who always doubled my money but that I didn't let him invest for me anymore, you would think I was foolish. The master let the first two stewards keep the money in their control.

What about the last steward, who was given only one talent? The master must have had reason not to entrust him with any more than he did. This servant hid the one talent and simply returned it to his master. He didn't even earn any interest on the money. *You ought therefore to have put my money to the exchangers, and then at my coming, I should have received mine own with usury* (Matt. 25:27). The interest on $2,000,000 after one year (or as stated in Matt. 25:19 *...after a long time)* at 8% is $160,000. His master became upset and went so far as to take the talent he had and gave it to the steward who already had 10 talents. Why did he take it away? Because it was costing him. The steward was unprofitable.

This concept is hard for some Christians to accept. Somehow, we have been encouraged to believe that God would never do anything like that. God isn't Robin Hood. He is not trying to find a way to tell successful people that they should be ashamed of their success. Rather, God wants to reinforce success in order to strengthen the principle of stewardship. God is trying to build His kingdom on earth through the hands of selfless servants who live with the realization that what they have belongs to God. How can we be sure that we don't lose sight of our stewardship and remain in a faithful position to live in the favor of our Master, who gave us the power to get wealth in the first place?

Step one is to tithe. Don't play around and give a little here and there to ease your conscience. Pay your tithes (10%). You don't give a tithe; you pay it. Why? Because you owe it. You give offerings. You can't give what you owe. You can only give what you don't owe (offerings).

Malachi 3:8
Will a man rob God? Yet you have robbed Me. But you say, Wherein have we robbed You? In tithes and offerings.

It is the consistent tither who is continually saying to his Master and to himself, "What I have is because of God's grace." For you to prosper on 90% of what your neighbor makes requires a life of faith in the covenant of God.

Malachi 3:10
Bring you all the tithes into the storehouse, that there may be meat in My house, and **prove Me** now herewith, says the Lord of hosts, if I will not open you the windows of heaven, and pour you out a blessing, that there shall not be room enough to receive it.

When it works and He prospers you, your faith is strengthened and the covenant is established.

How do you become the steward that the Master trusts with more and more? I want to use an analogy of how to move into deeper levels of confidence with your Master. When we tithe, it is like paying rent on our lives. All we have and all we are is from God. Tithing says, "I recognize that You are the rightful owner and I am paying what You require of me to reaffirm that my life is not my own." As God sees that we are internalizing the Kingdom's concepts and have made serious moves toward stewardship, from time to time, He will call upon us to **give** offerings.

Luke 6:38
Give, and it shall be given unto you; good measure, pressed down, and shaken together, and running over, shall men give into your bosom. For with the same measure that you meet withal it shall be measured to you again.

Remember, you only give when you participate in offerings, not just in tithing (Malachi 3:8-12). Why does God want offerings if we are already faithfully tithing? Offerings are opportunities to invest in the company. Obviously, the returns are greater on an investment than they would be by paying rent. It is God's way of saying, "Have you crossed over to see the value of investing in the Kingdom? Come into partnership with Me and help Me build the Kingdom."

If God is going to run the company, I would certainly like to participate in the profits. When seeing the Kingdom come on earth is important enough that you willingly invest in its future, a wonderful freedom from the cares of this world settles on you. Remember, stewardship says it doesn't matter who owns it as long as you get to use it when you need it. If I offered you the keys to a new Mercedes and said that you could use it whenever you wanted, would you be bitter because you didn't own it? When we learn the joy of stewardship under God's ownership, we are free indeed.

King David--God's Steward

Remember Deut. 17:14-20 says that the king should not multiply horses, gold, or silver **unto himself**. But we know from Scripture that Israel under King David was a wealthy nation. David himself was a wealthy man. That's how we see it. The important thing, however, is how did God see it, and how did David see it? In I Chronicles 29:1, when it was time for the house of the Lord to be built, David stepped forward. He indicated his desire to build God a house, but it wasn't meant to be. Solomon, David's son, was the one chosen to oversee the actual construction. David gathered all the chosen of Israel to reaffirm that Solomon was to build the house.

After this announcement, David revealed his heart when he said, *Now I have prepared with all my might for the house of my God...* (I Chronicles 29:2a). It was David himself, not Solomon, who had set aside all the gold, silver, timber, stone, brass, etc. necessary to build the temple (I Chronicles 29:2b). Everything that was needed was stored in the warehouses of Israel. No mortgage was required; all was ready.

The king's heart was harnessed to the Kingdom. David had long ago stopped renting and began investing. He was confident that his master was aware of his stewardship. What need was there to heap up for himself? He had come to understand the Kingdom. In fact, God's testimony of David was ...*I have found David the son of Jesse, a man after My own heart, who shall fulfill all My will* (Acts 13:22b).

David had given hundreds of millions of dollars in materials to insure that the temple was going to be the best it could be. But he wasn't finished yet. After all this, out of his love and appreciation for the Kingdom, he said he wanted to make an investment (offering) amounting to an additional 1.2 billion dollars.

Chronicles 29:3-4
Moreover, because I have set my affection to the house of my God, I have of mine own proper good, of gold and silver, which I have given to the house of my God, over and above all that I have prepared for the holy house, even three thousand talents of gold, of the gold of Ophir, and seven thousand talents of refined silver, to overlay the walls of the house withal.

You see, David had indeed heaped up large amounts of wealth, but not unto himself. God will prosper kings, but not just so they can live comfortable lives. They are holders of wealth for God's future purposes.

Israel was so moved that day that the leaders (other men serving on the king's side) in response to David's challenge to them, gave an additional 1.8 billion dollars themselves (I Chronicles 29:6-9). Not a bad day's offering! The kings go to war and spoil the enemies of God. Wealth accumulates for God's future purposes. That day the stewards released the wealth. This allowed the priests from that day forward to focus on their ministry to God and to the people without being drawn off course by the lack of money. Lack many times can pervert the plans of God far more quickly than prosperity.

Ask yourself this question. Was Joseph out of the will of God storing up grain for seven years? Certainly not. Once he had the grain stored, was he out of the will of God selling the grain and taking the wealth of Egypt? Certainly not. Priests would have given the food away. However, kings have a call as stewards to operate under a different anointing, and for good reason.

Kings--Men of the Word

Back to Deut. 17:14-20. The Word says that kings are to make a copy of the Law and to keep it with them always that they might meditate in it day and night so that they won't forget their God. Why would God want the kings to study the Law if He had priests? If a steward is going to represent God, then he should certainly know the Word. Kings are to be in partnership with priests and operate out of mutual respect.

I strongly believe that our Bible schools should offer training for kings. If churches had an army of Word-trained, warring kings who were full of faith and the Holy Ghost, I don't know how a pastor could not want and appreciate them being on the team. When pastors hear from God and revival comes, one of the first problems to surface is a lack of space.

The pastor says, "Where do we put the people?"

Wouldn't it be wonderful to have trained men who could hear from God and respond appropriately?

A knowledgeable king might say, "Don't be concerned pastor. We have prepared with all our might for the house of our God. We bought silver three years ago when it was down in price, and now it's up. We bought some real estate four years ago that has doubled in price. Our stocks are up.

"We have been listening to God for several years now and making preparation, and by listening to you, we knew that this day would come. We have mixed our faith with yours. It hasn't been easy, but we have resisted the devil. We haven't squandered our success on our own lusts. We have been waiting for God to tell us what to do with His wealth. Now don't concern yourself with all of the building details. We are fully prepared. You stay before God and lead us to further conquests in the pursuit of the souls of men.

"We will build the buildings. We will deal with the contractors. And we have taken up some extra offerings to further invest in the Kingdom we believe in. You need some more priests to help train all these new believers. Don't worry about us. We are with you. As soon as this project is finished, we will prepare again for the next expansion of the Kingdom."

Now tell me what pastor would not want that group of men in his church? Do you think he would be wise to encourage them to forsake their gift and study for years to become a choir leader or a youth director? God gifts and anoints choir leaders and youth directors. You don't make them by sending gifted kings off to Bible school.

It's time that we expanded our options. *Be kindly affectioned one to another with brotherly love; in honor preferring one another...* (Romans 12:10). The Kingdom will certainly advance when the kings come back to the Kingdom and are welcomed by the priests. Neither can find fulfillment without the other.

Can a King Be Anointed to Share the Word?

On a recent mission outreach to West Africa, I was privileged to minister in the area of economic development. For several days, I taught the financial principles of the Scripture to pastors and elders from over 25 churches. On the last day, one of the pastors came to me with an astonished look on his face. He said, "Never have we heard a businessman share the Word with such an anointing."

Remember, to be anointed, all you have to do is what God told you to do. When kings share from the Word about their office, they should move in the anointing of God. After all, according to Deut. 17, they are to be lifelong students of the Word.

Deut. 17:19
And it shall be with him, and he shall read therein all the days of his life; that he may learn to fear the Lord his God, to keep all the words of this law and these statutes, to do them.

We have thought too long that the only anointing rested on the five-fold ministry. Since that was the only place honor and recognition was given, everybody wanted to serve there. As we come to understand that kings are men of the Word and operate under the full anointing of heaven to serve where they are called, more members of the body will step forward to serve in offices that have for too long been vacated. The more complete the body is; the more effective it will be.

I Cor. 12:12, 28

For as the body is one, and has many members, and all the members of that one body, being many, are one body; so also is Christ.

And God has set some in the Church, first apostles, secondarily prophets, thirdly teachers, after that miracles, then gifts of healings, **helps, governments,** diversities of tongues.

Romans 12:8

Or he who exhorts, on exhortation; he who **gives** let him do it with simplicity; he who **rules** with diligence; he who shows mercy, with cheerfulness.

Cultural Conquest

For all the evangelism that has occurred since Jesus left the earth, you would think that more of the world would be saved. If we add up all the numbers that all the Christian ministries claim as converts, the world has already been saved. Obviously, the world is not yet won, so what is the problem? Where are all the converts? It is time that we as Christians ask ourselves some hard questions about our long term effectiveness.

In the parable of the sower in Matthew 13:23, the seed was sown but not all the seed endured until the crop was produced. The seed was sown, but with different results:

1. <u>Some fell by the wayside and the birds got them.</u>

These hear the Word, but it never gets down into their understanding; therefore, there is no positive response. Before they have a chance to even believe, other things distract them.

2. <u>Some fell on stony ground and had shallow roots.</u>

This group hears the Word, and before they truly deeply understand the whole message of the Kingdom, their emotions begin to run away with them. Many of us wait so desperately to be loved and forgiven that our emotions lead our response to the Word. This group's highs are higher than anyone else, and their lows are lower than any else. Because the true understanding of the Kingdom is set aside by this shallow response on the emotional level, when hard times come, there is nothing there to keep the faith. Even though these appear to have a genuine experience, time and hard times prove something to be lacking, as they pull back from the fervent zeal they had at the beginning.

3. <u>Some sprung up and the thorns choked them out.</u>

This group seems to have a genuine response. They hear the Word, and it appears that they have every intention to follow through with their decision. Somewhere along the way, however, the day to day pressures of just living begin to drain away the intensity of their commitment. As much as they want to do what they committed to do, something more important is always demanding their attention. Eventually, their first love loses out to neglect. The end result is the same as the first two responses. The only difference is that it takes a little longer before the message of the Kingdom becomes ineffective.

4. <u>Some fell on good soil and brought forth 100, 60 and 30 fold.</u>

When the Word of God finds a hungry heart that sincerely responds to heaven's call, spiritual understanding explodes. The heart attitudes of these true believers resonates with the opportunity to give away what they have just received. The reality of their newfound relationship with the God of heaven, compels them to share the Good News with all their world. They become witnesses of what they have experienced. As a result, others discover the same peace with God.

These various returns on the seed sown can tell us much about the effectiveness of different ministries. While evangelists sow much seed, few of them stay around long enough to watch over the seed to see it come to maturity. They are primarily counting on the fourth group. There are always some who hear the Word, and nothing will deter them from coming to maturity. Those who have the fourth response immediately fall in love with the heavenly message and stay the course, while the Kingdom grows up inside them, and they themselves begin to bear fruit. If not for these self starters and determined seekers, the evangelist would see little fruit.

In fact, most evangelistic ministries see the responses of categories two and three along with four and believe that all who walk the aisle or raise the hand will somehow follow through with their commitment. But we know from the parable that this simply is not true. By sowing the seed and simply leaving it, the harvest will not be three out of four, but rather, one out of four.

Simple mathematics tells us that if we think we are 75% effective when we are really only 25% effective, we have the feeling of winning; but we are, in fact, losing. Darkness is quite happy with the status quo. If this is even a fairly accurate representation of our effectiveness, then something quite different is required if we are ever to make major inroads into the strongholds that enslave this world's lost and needy.

What would it take to reverse the situation? In the Scripture, the failure of the seed sown on stony ground (#2) was due to misplaced over-enthusiasm. When difficulties arose, there wasn't enough understanding for the initial commitment to sustain the life of the seed of the Gospel. The seed sown that was attacked by thorns (#3) indicates that the importance of the decision to receive the good news of the Gospel simply gets shoved aside by the many demands of life. I don't know if you see this the way I do or not, but it seems to me that in this illustration, the major enemy of the Gospel is not the devil. In the parable, the devil is only directly involved in the first of the four categories of seeds sown. He just out and out comes and steals the Word before the hearer understands it. The Word never has a chance to penetrate the hearer's understanding; so those seeds never sprout.

By attacking the devil who only directly controls 25% of the seed and ignore or downplay the cause of the failure of the other 50% to come to maturity, we may be missing a tremendous opportunity to increase the harvest of the seed sprouted in categories two and three. So what is the cause of the failure of the 50% (#'s 2 & 3)? I believe the world or rather the "culture" of the world draws away twice as many people as the devil does directly. Most of the maintenance preaching, teaching, training, and counseling of churches is aimed at taking the evangelist's supposed 75% success and keeping as many of the new converts as possible.

Having pastored for approximately 25 years, I know that 90% of my time was consumed by 10% of my people, most of whom eventually strayed away no matter how much effort was made to help them "make it." As these few consumed all I had to give, I would occasionally look up from time to time to realize that many others had simply wondered off due to lack of interest. Over the years, there have been large numbers of people who seemed to have a real faith only to leave the faith and return to an unfruitful life. For years I asked myself what was wrong and how I was failing my flock.

Now that I have had a few years to step back and take notice, the answer seems quite simple. The draw of culture is so strong that people will over and over again make short-term decisions due to fear, excitement, survival, need for acceptance, etc. and will set the Gospel aside. Basically, the Church strongly believes in fighting the devil, but when it comes to fighting culture, we seem to cave in.

Oh, we are quick to preach against the dark side of our society. Any good pastor has a briefcase full of messages meant to persuade the flock not to drink, smoke, cuss, or go to dirty movies. The problem is that technology is running faster to deliver ease of sin and the cares of this world than we are running to respond to it.

In the Western World, the masses struggle to keep the lust of the flesh and cares of life from smothering the clear call of the Gospel. In the Third World, the struggle to survive causes the decision made last night at the crusade to withdraw in the sunlight of the hard realities of making a living and providing for families in very tightly closed societies. If culture can't entertain the decision away in the Western World, it threatens survival in the Third World. How can the priests properly address these challenges without the support and backing of the kings?

I believe it is clearly time for some radical changes in strategies for keeping the harvest reaped by the evangelists. If kings were to rise to the occasion and remove the rocks and cut out the thorns, how much more of the harvest could we keep? Just today, as I was able to share the Gospel with a young Muslim man in a West African country, his response was typical. After I carefully explained the difference between Mohammed and Jesus, I asked him if he understood. He said he did. I then asked if he believed what I had told him.

He said, "You have spoken the truth to me. I agree with you." I then asked if he would like to receive Christ, have his sins forgiven, and have his name written in the book of life. His response was typical. He said, "I am a Muslim. My family is Muslim. I work for a Muslim. I must provide for my family."

Even though he clearly understood the Gospel message, the threat that he would be considered an outcast and not be able to survive in this life kept him from making the right decision about the life to come. If the economy of his country was controlled by God's kings rather than Muslim businessmen, culture may not have won.

Rather than preaching against the problems, what do you think would happen if we began providing alternatives? I am not naive enough to believe that we will ever win every time. However, wouldn't it be nice to see some positive alternatives for a change? Rather than complaining about all the rotten movies, let's put some muscle behind our dissatisfaction and create movies that are uplifting, morally encouraging, and spiritually challenging.

Rather than complaining about the video games children are playing with all the killing and violence, let's make some games that teach the right things, like the principles of the Word of God.

Rather than complaining about Walt Disney's decline into humanism, evolutionism, and spiritualism, why not create a family entertainment complex that extols the glories of the Kingdom to come?

Rather than languish under the economic servitude of mortgages and high utility bills, why not believe God for witty inventions that will transition wealth and give economic independence to the Christian community?

Rather than complaining about the condition of our educational system, why not develop curriculums ourselves that will challenge and motivate young believers to excel intellectually so they might rise to leadership positions?

Rather than watching the Third World harvest wither, why not take real investment opportunities and jobs to those who need them and watch as the standard of living is raised and the economic power within these nations makes a shift to God's kingdom?

If by these and other culture changing moves the kings can remove some of the stones and cut down some of the thorns, then the success rate of the pastors should begin to see some positive changes. Teamwork has an opportunity to touch the 50% of the seed that has already taken root but needs serious attention to survive.

I believe some exciting days have arrived for the Church. As we now move into cultural conquest, we have the great privilege of shifting the effectiveness of the Gospel preached from 25% toward keeping the 75% who positively respond to the Word. In a short period of time, when we begin keeping more of the harvest than we are losing, the world will begin to look different.

2 Chr. 31:1-12 , 20-21

1   Now when all this was finished, all Israel that were present went out to the cities of Judah, and brake the images in pieces, and cut down the groves, and threw down the high places and the altars out of all Judah and Benjamin, in Ephraim also and Manasseh, until they had utterly destroyed them all. Then all the children of Israel returned, every man to his possession, into their own cities.

2   And Hezekiah appointed the courses of the priests and the Levites after their courses, every man according to his service, the priests and Levites for burnt offerings and for peace offerings, to minister, and to give thanks, and to praise in the gates of the tents of the LORD.

3   He appointed also <u>the king's portion of his substance</u> for the burnt offerings, to wit, for the morning and evening burnt offerings, and the burnt offerings for the Sabbaths, and for the new moons, and for the set feasts, as it is written in the law of the LORD.

4   Moreover he commanded the people that dwelt in Jerusalem <u>to give the portion of the priests and the Levites, that they might be encouraged</u> in the law of the LORD.

5   And as soon as the commandment came abroad, the children of Israel brought in abundance the firstfruits of corn, wine, and oil, and honey, and of all the increase of the fields; and the tithe of all things brought they in abundantly.

6   And concerning the children of Israel and Judah, that dwelt in the cities of Judah, they also brought in the tithe of oxen and sheep, and the tithe of holy things which were consecrated unto the LORD their God, and laid them by heaps.

7   In the third month they began to lay the foundation of the heaps, and finished them in the seventh month.

8   And when Hezekiah and the princes came and saw the heaps, they blessed the LORD, and his people Israel.

9   Then Hezekiah questioned with the priests and the Levites concerning the heaps.

10   And Azariah the chief priest of the house of Zadok answered him, and said, <u>Since the people began to bring the offerings into the house of the LORD, we have had enough to eat, and have left plenty: for the LORD has blessed his people; and that which is left is this great store.</u>

11   Then Hezekiah commanded to prepare chambers in the house of the LORD; and they prepared them,

12   And brought in the offerings and the tithes and the dedicated things faithfully: over which Cononiah the Levite was ruler, and Shimei his brother was the next.

20   And thus did Hezekiah throughout all Judah, and wrought that which was good and right and truth before the LORD his God.

21   And in every work that he began in the service of the house of God, and in the law, and in the commandments, to seek his God, <u>he did it with all his heart, and prospered.</u>

Summary

Have you ever wondered why all the money seems to be in the world's hands? Why are all the technological innovations marketed to us by corporations who seem unresponsive to the real need of the world to know God? These questions have haunted me for years. I have asked myself over and over, "Why can't the Church lead for a change?"

It is in pursuit of these answers that God has led my life to the difference He promised that five year-old boy. Today, doors of opportunity have opened to serve the Kingdom in a global, economic strategy to see the Kingdom advance. We live in a day when bigger church buildings and more benevolence to hurting people through charity programs are not going to get the job done.

You may have noticed in recent years that strong, mature ministries are standing up with plans for global evangelization. For these plans to succeed, the king's side of the Kingdom must stand with like commitment to the cause. Kings must live with the same dedication, sacrifice, and long-term planning that will provide the bridge to transfer wealth from the world to God's cause. If the wealth of the wicked is laid up for the just, God must anoint someone to go after it.

That is my life's call. The days of lack must give way by application of divine economics to see provision pursue and overtake the vision. As God has blessed my wife and me to travel the world in pursuit of His unfolding plan, it has been our great joy to see many respond to these new areas of service.

The door stands open for applicants. Anyone who has the inward witness may apply. Can women serve as kings? I am sure you noticed this book was written with a male slant. That's the way it flowed out of my heart.

The Scripture says that it is God's will that all **men** be saved. Does that mean that God didn't want women to be saved? Of course not. Surely by now we are all mature enough to know that in Christ there is neither male nor female. Consider the lives of Deborah, Ruth, Esther, Pricilla, and Dorcas to see if their services fit more on the king's side or on the priest's side.

Whoever you are, Jew or Greek, bond or free, male or female, if you have heard from God and move toward

His will, there is where you will find His grace and anointing.

My sincere prayer is that your heart has been opened and that you might see a broader area of service to God. Kings shouldn't be made to feel second class. They are called by God to their duties. Kings, the world seriously needs your gift. The priests seriously need your gift. May God bless you in your personal quest to find your place in His body. Once you find it, serve with all your heart.

I Chronicles 29:2

Now I have prepared with all my might for the house of my God.